BIGGEST NAMES IN SPORTS
ODELL BECKHAM JR.
FOOTBALL STAR

by Marty Gitlin

Focus
READERS

North Star
EDITIONS

WWW.NORTHSTAREDITIONS.COM

Produced for North Star Editions by Red Line Editorial.

Photographs ©: Evan Pinkus/AP Images, cover, 1; Julio Cortez/AP Images, 4–5; Phalen M. Ebenhack/AP Images, 7; Seth Poppel/Yearbook Library, 8–9, 11, 12; John Albright/Icon Sportswire, 14; Jonathan Bachman/AP Images, 16–17; Gerald Herbert/AP Images, 19, 20; Seth Wenig/AP Images, 22–23; Kevin Terrell/AP Images, 25; Kirby Lee/NFL/AP Images, 26; Red Line Editorial, 29

ISBN
978-1-63517-038-2 (hardcover)
978-1-63517-094-8 (paperback)
978-1-63517-196-9 (ebook pdf)
978-1-63517-146-4 (hosted ebook)

Library of Congress Control Number: 2016951014

Printed in the United States of America
Mankato, MN
November, 2016

ABOUT THE AUTHOR

Marty Gitlin is a sportswriter and educational book author based in Cleveland, Ohio. He has had more than 100 books published, including dozens about famous athletes.

TABLE OF CONTENTS

CHAPTER 1

THE CATCH

On November 23, 2014, the New York Giants hosted the Dallas Cowboys. Millions of fans were watching the Sunday Night Football clash. But none could have guessed what they were about to see.

The Giants led 7–3. On the first play of the second quarter, Giants quarterback Eli Manning dropped back to pass.

Beckham's amazing catch was the talk of the football world for weeks.

He heaved the ball to rookie wide receiver Odell Beckham Jr. Cowboys cornerback Brandon Carr covered Beckham closely as they sprinted down the right sideline. Near the end zone, Beckham leaped into the air. He stretched his right arm as high and far back as he could. He was falling backward. But he somehow snagged the ball with just his fingertips. Then he fell into the end zone for a touchdown.

The television announcers said Beckham had made one of the greatest catches of all time. It would be hard to argue with that. But talent alone did not allow Beckham to make the play. He practiced catching one-handed before

Beckham practices one-handed catches as he warms up before games.

every game. He knew he could do it.
And his confidence grew with each
great catch.

The Giants lost that game to Dallas.
But Beckham had become a superstar
that night. And he would only get better.

CHAPTER 2

BOY WITH A DREAM

When Odell Beckham Jr. was four years old, his mother asked him what he wanted to be when he grew up. He was tossing around a football at their home in New Orleans, Louisiana. Odell replied that he would play in the National Football League (NFL) someday.

Odell knew when he was just a little kid that he wanted to be a pro football player.

Those childhood dreams don't come true for most people. But Odell was not like most kids. He was driven toward a football career. And he worked hard to make his dream come true.

He had the right parents for the job. His father was a running back at Louisiana State University (LSU) in Baton Rouge, Louisiana. His mother was a track star at LSU. His parents brought Odell to their classes when he was a baby.

Odell wanted to be more than a good **athlete**. He wanted to be a great one. His parents knew how much sweat and **dedication** that required. They guided their son every step of the way.

Odell slashes through the defense while playing for Isidore Newman School.

Football wasn't Odell's only sport. He began playing soccer when he was three. He was a standout basketball player at Isidore Newman School in New Orleans.

Odell was a football star in high school, but he also played basketball and ran track.

And he earned a spot at the state track meet in the long jump and 200-meter dash. But he did not let go of his dream. He emerged as one of the top young football players in the country.

Odell usually played wide receiver. On some downs, he played running back or quarterback. He also played defensive back. But Odell was mostly a receiver. He totaled 1,110 receiving yards and 15 touchdowns as a senior. He became Newman's first 1,000-yard receiver in 20 years. In one game, he erupted for 212 yards and four touchdowns.

Odell had **scholarship** offers from several colleges. But he decided to stay close to home. He followed in his parents' footsteps and went to LSU.

His dream of playing in the NFL was closer than ever. He drove himself to make sure he had the best chance to achieve it.

Odell played in a national high school all-star game before he left for LSU.

Beckham worked endlessly on running perfect routes and making sharp cuts to break free from defensive backs. He practiced his footwork. He stretched to catch every pass within reach. He studied great NFL receivers such as Victor Cruz and DeSean Jackson. He displayed the work ethic needed to grow into greatness.

Beckham worked so hard that he earned playing time as a freshman at LSU. He improved as a sophomore. By his junior year, Beckham was one of the best college football players in the country. He was about to become a star.

HIGH SCHOOL ROYALTY

Beckham was not the first NFL superstar to play football at Isidore Newman School. Famed quarterbacks Peyton and Eli Manning attended the school before Beckham arrived on campus. Beckham attended the Manning Passing Academy—the clinic put on by the Manning family—two years in a row. He got to catch passes from the Manning brothers. Little did he know that he would soon be catching a lot more of Eli Manning's passes.

CHAPTER 3

SUPER SEASON

Odell Beckham Jr. blossomed in 2013. Many **scouts** thought the LSU junior was among the most improved players in college football. He caught 59 passes for 1,152 yards. He scored eight touchdowns. That doubled his total from the previous two years combined.

Beckham leaps over a Furman defender to catch a touchdown pass in a 2013 game.

His hard work had paid off. He was now a confident player. He burst off the line with quickness. Scouts raved about his route running. They loved his ability to make tough catches. They praised him as a threat to score after catching the ball.

Beckham had one great game after another. He scored three touchdowns against Alabama–Birmingham. He caught nine passes for 179 yards and two scores against Mississippi State. He racked up a career-best 204 yards against Furman.

Beckham had plenty of help as well. In 2013, he and fellow wide receiver Jarvis Landry became the first pair of teammates in LSU history to each top

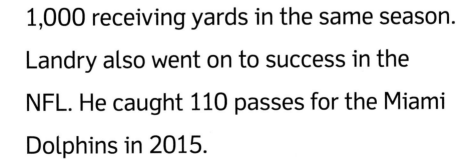

Beckham lunges to catch a pass against Washington.

1,000 receiving yards in the same season. Landry also went on to success in the NFL. He caught 110 passes for the Miami Dolphins in 2015.

Beckham slashes through the Florida defense in 2013.

Beckham's performance in 2013 earned him plenty of praise. He won the Paul Hornung Award. That honor is given every year to the most **versatile** player in the country. Beckham was expected to be taken early in the 2014 NFL **draft**. The only mystery was which team would grab him. The New York Giants chose Beckham with the 12th pick in the first round.

The Giants would not regret their pick. After a slow and painful start, Beckham was simply incredible.

FAMILY TIES

Having a track coach for a mother has helped Beckham in his own career. Beckham's mother, Heather Van Norman, gave him advice about running form and how to start the 40-yard dash quickly. She gave him pointers before NFL teams scouted him. In 2012 Van Norman was named track coach at Nicholls State University.

CHAPTER 4

BIG HEART, BIG TALENT

Rookies dream about making a big splash. But Odell Beckham Jr.'s dream began as a nightmare. He injured his **hamstring** on the first day of his first training camp in 2014. He returned to the Giants a few weeks later, but then he hurt his hamstring again.

Beckham scores his first NFL touchdown in a 2014 game against the Atlanta Falcons.

Beckham missed the first four weeks of the regular season. But eventually he ran wild. He became the second player in league history with at least 90 receiving yards in nine straight games. He averaged an incredible nine catches and 133 yards per game during that stretch. He also scored nine touchdowns.

Beckham was voted NFL Offensive Rookie of the Year in 2014. And he improved in his second year. Some players slip after great rookie seasons. But his work ethic and desire to be the best would not allow it.

Beckham followed the same trend in 2015. He started slowly with just two

Beckham has the Giants' passing game pointed in the right direction.

100-yard efforts in his first seven games. But then he averaged 133 receiving yards over the next six games. He scored nine touchdowns during a seven-game period. He finished the season with 1,450 receiving yards.

College teammates Beckham (left) and Landry exchanged jerseys after the Giants beat the Dolphins in 2015.

Beckham did it with talent. He also did it with heart and desire. On the day of a game in Miami, he was so sick with a stomach virus that the Giants' medical staff gave him three bags of fluids through an IV. Yet he still racked up 166 yards and two touchdowns to help his team beat the Dolphins and Jarvis Landry, his college teammate.

Perhaps that desire is to be expected. After all, it has been burning in him since he was four years old.

RELATED BY TALENT

Odell Beckham is a huge fan of soccer superstar David Beckham. And that's not just because they share the same last name. Odell grew up playing soccer. David Beckham was one of his idols. Odell often joked about being related to David. The two finally met in 2015. Odell talked about how excited he was to meet his soccer hero.

ODELL BECKHAM JR.

- Height: 5 feet 11 inches (180 cm)
- Weight: 198 pounds (90 kg)
- Birth date: November 5, 1992
- Birthplace: New Orleans, Louisiana
- High school: Isidore Newman
- College: Louisiana State University, Baton
  Rouge, Louisiana (2011–2013)
- NFL team: New York Giants (2014–)
- Major awards: NFL Offensive Rookie of the
  Year 2014

New York

Baton Rouge

New Orleans

FOCUS ON
ODELL BECKHAM JR.

Write your answers on a separate piece of paper.

1. Write a sentence that describes the key ideas in this book.

2. Beckham wanted to go to the same college where his parents had been star athletes. Would you want to do the same thing? Why or why not?

3. Which player was Beckham's teammate on the LSU football team?

    A. Eli Manning
    B. Jarvis Landry
    C. Sammy Watkins

4. What helped Beckham develop the skills needed to win the Paul Hornung Award?

    A. studying many of the great NFL receivers
    B. going to the same university as his parents
    C. playing several different positions in high school

Answer key on page 32.

GLOSSARY

athlete
A person who plays a sport.

dedication
Strong commitment.

draft
A system that allows teams to acquire new players coming into a league.

hamstring
A tendon located at the back of the upper leg.

scholarship
Money given to a student to pay for education expenses.

scouts
People whose jobs involve looking for talented young players.

versatile
Able to do a number of things well.

TO LEARN MORE

BOOKS

Jacobs, Greg. *The Everything Kids' Football Book: All-Time Greats, Legendary Teams, and Today's Favorite Players—with Tips on Playing like a Pro.* Avon, MA: Adams Media, 2014.

Mack, Larry. *The New York Giants Team Story.* Minneapolis: Bellwether Media, 2016.

Silverman, Drew. *Today's NFL: 12 Reasons Fans Follow the Game.* North Mankato, MN: 12-Story Library, 2016.

NOTE TO EDUCATORS

Visit **www.focusreaders.com** to find lesson plans, activities, links, and other resources related to this title.

INDEX